CROCK POT DUMP MEALS

By:

KATYA JOHANSSON

« Introduction »

Dump meals are super simple recipes, that require one minute to plan and a few extra minutes to assemble. The process is pretty straighforwrd: you simply dump all the ingredients into your slow cooker or pressure cooker, let them cook while you go about your busy life and Enjoy heavenly suppers and treats afterwards. Pretty cool, right?

This simple concept makes planning dinners less demanding than at any other time. Every recipe in CrockPot Dump Meals Cookbook is rather simple and it usually only takes up to five minutes to get the dish ready. Just dump the ingredients into your crockpot and let it do all the work for you.

Enjoy!

Contents

1. Beef with Healthy Carrots

Ingredients

- 4 – 5 Lbs. of Beef Chuck Roast
- 2 Cups of Beef Broth
- 1/2 Cup Light Brown Sugar
- 1/4 Cup Balsamic Vinegar
- 1 Tbls of Soy Sauce
- 1 Tsp of Salt
- 1/4 Tsp of Red Pepper Flakes
- 3 Cloves of Fresh Garlic – Pressed
- Zest of 1/2 an Orange
- Red Potatoes – Washed

Method

1. Place Meat and Potatoes inside the crockpot and turn on low heat.
2. Whisk together all the other ingredients and pour over the top of the meat. Cook on low for 6-8 hours
3. Serve with some Mashed Potatoes. Enjoy!

2. Slow Cooker Delicious Vegetable Stew

Ingredients

- 1 large white onion OR 2 leeks (white parcel just), slashed
- 1 lb. butternut squash, peeled, seeded and slashed
- 1 lb. carrots, peeled and slashed
- 1 lb. parsnips, peeled and slashed
- 1 lb. sweet potatoes, peeled and slashed
- 1 lb. (Yukon Gold) potatoes, peeled and slashed
- 2 celery ribs, stems evacuated and slashed
- 6 cloves garlic, peeled and finely cut
- 3 glasses chicken or vegetable stock
- 1 narrows leaf
- 1 Tbsp. crisp sage leaves, finely slashed
- 1 tsp. naturally split dark pepper
- 1/2 tsp. ocean salt
- 2 glasses slashed new kale
- Optional: sage leaves for topping

Method

1. Add all the ingredients except the kale into a slow cooker, and precisely blend to consolidate.
2. Cook on low heat for 6-8 hours until the vegetables are delicate.
3. Expel narrows leaf, and precisely mix in the kale. Give the stew a chance to keep cooking for 10 minutes or so until the kale is shriveled. Season with extra salt and pepper if need be. Turn off slow cooker.
4. Serve instantly, with the choice to decorate with sage leaves or Parmesan cheddar.

3. Delicious Country Style BBQ Ribs

Ingredients

- 2-3 lbs. boneless pork nation style ribs
- 1/2 expansive onion, finely cut
- 3 cloves garlic, minced
- 1/4 glass cocoa sugar
- 1/2 glass fruit purée
- 1/2 glasses grill sauce
- salt and pepper

Method

1. sprinkle salt and pepper on your boneless pork ribs on both sides.
2. Add all ingredients to your slow cooker. Delicately blend it all up. Cook on low for 5-6 hours.
3. At this point, expel the meat from the slow cooker. Dispose of juices. Top with 1/2 container crisp bbq sauce. Serve.

4. Ham and Delicious Bean Stew

Ingredients

- 1 lb. cooked ham, cut into 1/2-inch blocks (3 glasses)
- 1 glass dried naval force beans, sorted, flushed
- 2 medium stalks celery, cut (1 glass)
- 1 little onion, slashed (1/4 glass)
- 2 medium carrots, cut (1 glass)
- 2 glasses water
- 1/4 teaspoon dried thyme clears out
- 1/4 teaspoon fluid smoke
- 1/4 glass slashed new parsley

Method

1. In 3 1/2-to 4-quart slow cooker, blend all ingredients aside from parsley.
2. Cover; cook on Low heat setting 10 to 12 hours or until beans are delicate.
3. Blend in parsley before serving.

5. Amazing Honey sesame chicken

Ingredients

- 1 little onion, diced
- 2 cloves garlic, minced
- 1/2 glass nectar
- 1/2 glass soy sauce
- 1/4 glass ketchup
- 2 tablespoons vegetable oil
- 1/4 teaspoon pounded red pepper chips
- 2 pounds boneless, skinless chicken thighs
- Genuine salt and newly ground dark pepper, to taste
- 1 green onion, meagerly cut for enhancement
- Sesame seeds, for enhancement

Method

1. In a largedish, mix together onion, garlic, nectar, soy sauce, ketchup, vegetable oil and red pepper.
2. Season chicken thighs with salt and pepper, to taste. Place chicken thighs into a slow cooker. Include nectar blend and delicately hurl to join. Cover and cook on low heat for 3 hours and 30 minutes.
3. Expel chicken thighs from the slow cooker and shred the chicken before coming back to the pot with the juices. Cover and keep warm for an extra 30 minutes.
4. Serve quickly, embellished with green onions and sesame seeds, if craved.

6. Sweet Healthy Cashew Chicken

Ingredients

- 1 and 1/2 measures of Rice (we utilize chestnut rice, not the moment kind)
- Broccoli Crowns, daintily cleaved (or carrots < — that tastes super sweet as well!)
- 1/2 measure of diced onion.
- 3/4 measure of Cashews.
- 4 Chicken Boneless, Skinless Breasts
- 1 little jar of diced pineapple
- 1/some water

Method

1. Likewise with alternate formulas, layer the ingredients in your pack with the rice on the base and the chicken on top. At that point, cut the base of the pack to drop the ingredients into your stewing pot.
2. Pour your fluid (pineapple and water) over the chicken preceding turning on your slow cooker. Yummy! Your dinner will be prepared 6 hours or so later.

7. Chicken, Beans and Tasty Rice

Ingredients

- 1/2 measures of wild rice.
- 1/2 an onion diced
- 1 jar of pinto or red kidney beans
- 2 measures of chicken stock
- 1 jar of diced tomatoes
- Salt and Pepper to taste

Method

1. Layer your ingredients in your cooler zip lock pack. You will need the rice to be on the base, topped by the beans and chicken, then the fluids poured over the top.
2. The juices truly makes this formula healthy, don't skip it. Present with a side serving of mixed greens of blended greens

8. Amazing White Chicken Chili

Ingredients

- 4 Chicken Breasts
- 1 Onion, slashed
- 1 tsp. Minced Garlic
- 2 tsp. Ground Cumin
- 2 tsp. Oregano
- 2-3 jars Great Northern Beans
- 1 little can Chopped Green Chilies
- 2 jars Chicken Broth
- 12 oz. destroyed Monterey Jack Cheese

Method

1. Dump everything except for the juices and cheddar into your sack. The day of cooking pop the substance of your pack into your slow cooker and pour in the chicken stock.
2. Cook it on high for 6 or more hours. Just before serving, shred the chicken with two forks and blend in the cheddar. Serve this

9. Delicious creole chicken and wiener

Ingredients

- 1 pound boneless skinless chicken bosoms
- 12 ounces smoked Andouille wiener, cut into little adjusts
- 1 glass slashed onions
- 2 cloves minced garlic
- 1¼ glass low sodium chicken juices
- 1 can (14.5 ounces) diced tomatoes
- 3 tablespoons tomato glue
- ½ glass tomato sauce
- 2 teaspoons Creole flavoring
- ¼ teaspoon cayenne
- Optional additional items:
- 1 tablespoon cocoa sugar
- 1 14 ounce can dark beans, flushed and depleted
- 2 green ringer peppers, slashed
- ½ container cut green onions for fixing
- 2 tablespoons almond spread (haphazardly heavenly)
- salt to taste
- chestnut rice for serving

Method

1. Place the fundamental ingredients in the stewing pot. Cover and cook on low for 6-8 hours or high for 3 hours.
2. Shred the chicken specifically in the stewing pot to your sought surface. Include the additional items, on the off chance that you need, and cover and cook for another 20-30 minutes. This is additionally an incredible time to make your rice, in case you're serving it with rice.
3. At the point when everything is prepared, taste the chicken blend and season with salt. Serve the creole chicken over rice and finished with green onions.

10. Healthy Vegetarian Chili

Ingredients

- 1 glass uncooked farro or quinoa
- 1 medium red or yellow onion, peeled and diced
- 4 cloves of garlic, minced
- 1 chipotle bean stew in adobo sauce***, slashed
- 2 (15 ounce) jars dim red kidney beans, flushed and depleted (**see underneath for substitution thoughts)
- 2 (15 ounce) jars tomato sauce
- 2 (14 ounce) jars diced tomatoes
- 1 (15 ounce) can light red kidney beans, flushed and depleted
- 1 (4 ounce) can slashed green chilies
- 4 glasses vegetable stock
- 1 glass lager (or you can simply include additional vegetable soup)
- 2 Tablespoons bean stew powder
- 1 Tablespoon ground cumin
- 1 teaspoon salt
- 1 teaspoon sugar
- 1/2 teaspoon dark pepper
- (Optional garnishes: destroyed cheddar, pounded tortilla chips or strips, daintily cut green onions, sharp cream, salsa, and so on.)

Slow cooker method:

1. Add all ingredients to a slow cooker and blend altogether to join. Cook on high for 3-4 hours or on low for 6-8 hours until the stew is cooked through. Taste, and season with extra salt and pepper or seasonings if need be.
2. Serve quickly, embellished with additional garnishes if craved. Then again refrigerate in a fixed holder for up to 3 days, or stop for up to 3 months.

Stovetop method:

1. In a little pot, cook the farro or quinoa in the vegetable stock as per bundle headings until it is cooked through. (There will be additional vegetable stock - don't stress, you'll add everything to the bean stew once the farro/quinoa is cooked.)
2. In the interim as the farro/quinoa are cooking, heat 1 Tablespoon olive oil in a different vast stockpot over medium-high heat. Include your diced onions and sauté for 4-5 minutes until delicate and translucent. Include the majority of your remaining ingredients short the vegetable stock and farro (or quinoa), and mix to join. Keep cooking until the bean stew achieves a stew, then decrease heat to medium-low and stew for 10 minutes. Once the quinoa/farro is cooked, include it (alongside any additional vegetable stock) to the bean stew and blend to join. Taste, and season with extra salt and pepper or seasonings if need be.
3. Serve instantly, decorated with additional ingredients if sought. On the other hand refrigerate in a fixed compartment for up to 3 days, or stop for up to 3 months.

11. Honey-Garlic Chicken

Ingredients

- 4 boneless, skinless chicken thighs
- 4 garlic cloves, minced
- ¼ container nectar
- ½ container ketchup (you can likewise utilize low-sodium ketchup, if accessible)
- ½ container low sodium soy sauce
- ½ teaspoon dried oregano
- 2 tablespoons new parsley
- ½ tablespoon toasted sesame seeds

Method

1. Orchestrate chicken thighs on the base of your slow cooker; put aside.
2. In a blending dish, consolidate garlic, nectar, ketchup, soy sauce, oregano and parsley; rush until altogether joined.
3. Pour the sauce over the chicken thighs.
4. Close with a top and cook for 6 to 7 hours on LOW, or 4 to 5 hours on HIGH.*
5. Evacuate top and exchange chicken to a serving plate.
6. Spoon the sauce over the chicken and sprinkle with toasted sesame seeds.
7. Serve.

12. Mouthwatering LASAGNA

Ingredients

- 1 pound ground Italian wiener (I utilized zesty) or ground beef*
- 2 (24-ounce) jugs of good-quality Italian pasta sauce**
- 16 uncooked no-bubble lasagna noodles
- 32 ounces part-skim ricotta cheddar
- 2 mugs destroyed Mozzarella cheddar
- 1/2 glass ground Parmesan cheddar
- 2 mugs cleaved new child spinach
- 1/4 container finely-slashed crisp basil

Method

1. Include the ground Italian wiener (or ground hamburger) to a vast sauté container, and cook over medium-high heat until seared and cooked through, utilizing a largespoon to blend and separate the meet into little disintegrates as it cooks. Expel from heat and channel off any overabundance oil. Put aside.
2. In the interim, as the meat is cooking, simply ahead and inspire prepared to amass the lasagna. Start by showering the supplement of a large6-quart slow cooker with cooking splash. At that point layer the ingredients in the accompanying request:
3. Spread 1/2 mugs pasta sauce equally along the base of the slow cooker.
4. Layer around 4 lasagna noodles - breaking them into little pieces as expected to fit - uniformly over the sauce to cover the base of the slow cooker.
5. Layer around 1/3 of the ricotta cheddar (somewhat more than 1 container) uniformly on top of the noodles. (I discovered it was least demanding to do this in little spoonful, and after that spread them out with a spatula.

It's absolutely alright on the off chance that it's muddled and uneven!)

6. Sprinkle 1/2 measure of the destroyed Mozzarella cheddar and 2 Tablespoons of the Parmesan cheddar in an even layer on top of the ricotta.
7. Layer around 1/3 of the cooked ground meat in an even layer on top of the cheeses.
8. Layer around 1/3 of the slashed spinach in an even layer on top of the ground meat.
9. Layer 1 measure of pasta sauce in an even layer on top of the spinach.
10. Rehash with another layer of noodles, ricotta, Mozzarella/Parmesan, ground meat, spinach, and sauce. At that point rehash with another layer of noodles, ricotta, Mozzarella/Parmesan, ground meat, spinach, and sauce. At that point include one more layer of noodles, sauce, and Mozzarella.
11. Place the top on the slow cooker and cook on high for 3-4 hours or on low for 6-8 hours, or until the noodles are delicate.
12. Turn off the heat, and sprinkle the highest point of the lasagna equitably with the remaining Parmesan and crisp basil. Serve quickly. (Alternately on the off chance that you give the lasagna a chance to sit and rest for 30 minutes, it will cut into pieces significantly more effectively.)

13. Delicious Carnitas

Ingredients

- 4-5 lbs. pork shoulder
- 5 cloves garlic
- 1 tablespoon salt
- 1 teaspoon cumin
- 1 teaspoon bean stew powder
- 1 teaspoon dark pepper
- 1 teaspoon oregano
- ¼ teaspoon cinnamon
- ½ teaspoon cayenne pepper
- 1 tablespoon chipotle hot sauce (Optional)
- juice of 2 limes
- ½ container squeezed orange
- 12 ounces brew
- ½ container salsa (I jump at the chance to utilize a less thick one)

Method

1. Place the pork shoulder in the slow cooker. Generally hack the garlic and spot in the slow cooker (I really sort of rubbed it onto the meat to get however much garlic flavor as could reasonably be expected, yet you could simply hurl it in, as well).
2. Sprinkle the meat with salt, cumin, bean stew powder, dark pepper, oregano, cinnamon, and cayenne. Rub seasonings onto the pork.
3. Include lime juice, squeezed orange, lager, and salsa. Cover and cook on low for 8 hours.
4. Shred meat with two forks straightforwardly in the slow cooker (or take out, shred, and supplant in sauce). It ought to break apart effectively.
5. Preheat oven. Line a preparing sheet with aluminum foil. Place the destroyed meat on the cooking sheet and pour a

couple of spoonful of sauce over the top. Sear for 5-10 minutes or until you get sautéed edges on the pork.
6. Serve on tortillas with crisp cilantro, avocado, and lime juice.

14. Amazing Texas Chili

Ingredients

- 2 1/2 pounds hamburger toss, cut into 2-inch 3D squares
- 2 tablespoons pressed light chestnut sugar
- Fit salt
- 2 tablespoons vegetable oil
- 1 little onion, finely slashed
- 5 cloves garlic, crushed
- 2 4 .5-ounce jars slashed green chilies, depleted
- 1 tablespoon ground cumin
- 3/4 glass bean stew powder
- 1 14 - ounce can diced tomatoes with chilies
- 1 to 2 tablespoons green hot sauce
- Cut scallions, crisp cilantro and/or acrid cream, for fixing
- Tortilla chips, for serving (Optional)

Method

1. Hurl the hamburger with 1 tablespoon every chestnut sugar and salt in an extensive dish. Heat the vegetable oil in a huge skillet over medium-high heat. Cook the hamburger in bunches until sautéed on all sides, 4 to 5 minutes (don't swarm the container). Exchange to a 5-to-6-quart slow cooker.
2. Lessen the heat to medium, add the onion to the skillet and cook until delicate, around 5 minutes. Mix in the garlic, chilies, cumin and bean stew powder and cook 3 minutes. Include 1/2 mugs water and the tomatoes and stew, scratching up the caramelized bits from the base, around 3 minutes. Exchange to the slow cooker, cover and cook on low, 7 hours.
3. Include the remaining 1 tablespoon cocoa sugar and the hot sauce to the bean stew. Present with scallions, cilantro and/or acrid cream for fixing, and chips, if sought.

15. Healthy Peach Cobbler

Ingredients

- 6 ounces dull chestnut sugar
- 3 1/2 ounces moved oats
- 4 ounces generally useful flour
- 1/2 teaspoon preparing powder
- 1/2 teaspoon crisply ground allspice
- 1/2 teaspoon crisply ground nutmeg
- 1/4 teaspoon genuine salt
- 1/4 container unsalted spread, at room temperature, in addition to additional for the cooker
- 20 ounces solidified peach cuts

Method

1. Consolidate the sugar, oats, flour, preparing powder, allspice, nutmeg and legitimate salt in a vast dish. Include the spread and work into the dry ingredients until a brittle surface is framed. Fold in the peach cuts.
2. Spread the base and sides of a 3-quart cooker. Add the blend to the slow cooker and cook on low for 3 to 3 1/2 hours. Serve promptly.

16. Delicious Chicken Wild Rice Soup

Ingredients

- 1 glass uncooked wild rice
- 1 pound chicken bosoms
- 2 mugs mirepoix (cleaved celery, carrots, and onions)
- 6 mugs chicken stock
- 1 teaspoon poultry flavoring
- ½ glass margarine
- ¾ glass flour
- 2 mugs entire milk
- a couple of tablespoons white wine (Optional)
- up to 2 glasses extra drain or water

Method

1. Flush the wild rice. Place the uncooked wild rice, crude chicken, mirepoix, chicken juices, and poultry flavoring in a slow cooker. Cover and cook on low for 7-8 hours. The chicken ought to be cooked through and the rice ought to be delicate. There will be additional fluid in the simmering pot; don't deplete.
2. Expel the chicken bosoms from the simmering pot and permit to cool somewhat. Utilizing two forks, shred the chicken. Return the destroyed chicken to the simmering pot.
3. Whenever rice and chicken are done cooking, liquefy the spread in a pan. Include the flour and let the blend rise for 1 minute. Gradually race in the entire milk until a thick, smooth blend frames. Blend in the wine.
4. Add this to the rice and chicken in the stewing pot and blend to consolidate. Add additional water or drain to modify the consistency as you like it. Season with extra salt and pepper.

17. Delicious Roast with Gravy

Ingredients

- 2-3 tbsp. olive oil
- salt (ideally coarse salt like genuine)
- pepper
- 3 to 5 lb. hurl dish (could likewise utilize top or base round meal)
- 2 onions, peeled and cut down the middle
- 6-8 medium carrots, peeled and cut into 3-inch sticks
- 2 c. hamburger stock
- 1 tsp. dry pounded rosemary or 3-4 new rosemary sprigs
- 1 tsp. dried thyme or 2-3 crisp thyme sprigs

Method

1. Generously salt and pepper your meat on both sides.
2. In a substantial pot, heat olive oil over medium-high heat until extremely hot. Utilizing tongs, put your onion parts in the oil for around a moment on every side or just until cooked. Expel and put aside.
3. At that point put the carrots in the hot oil; move them around for around 2 minutes until marginally cooked. Evacuate and put aside. Add another tablespoon of oil to the pot, heat it again until exceptionally hot, and after that add your meat to the pot. Burn for around 1 minute on every side and afterward expel it.
4. With the burner still on high, include 1 c. of hamburger stock, whisking continually to deglaze your pot and get those tasty meat bits slackened from the base of the container. Turn heat off after around 1 minute.
5. Oil your stewing pot with cooking splash. Place your burned meat in, and after that toss in the onions and carrots. Pour the hamburger stock (the stock you used to deglaze the pot) over the meat...use enough to cover the meat about midway (you may need to utilize a percentage

of the extra meat stock that you didn't use for deglazing; in the event that you don't utilize everything, set the rest of the cooler for making the sauce later).

6. Sprinkle everything with the dry rosemary or thyme, ensuring the flavors get blended into the stock.
7. Spread the stewing pot and cook on high for around 4 hours (may require somewhat more time in case you're utilizing a 5-lb. broil).
8. You'll know your meal is done in the event that you can sever bits of meat with your fork.
9. Serve the meat with the carrots and onion cuts over some steaming pureed potatoes.

18. Amazing Meatball Vegetable Soup

Ingredients

- 1 pound little meatballs (locally acquired or custom made)
- 24oz container of pasta sauce (around 2.5 glasses)
- 4 containers low sodium chicken stock
- 1 pound carrots, peeled and hacked
- 3 containers green beans, closes cut off and cut into nibble estimated pieces
- 1 medium-sized zucchini, closes cut off and cut into chomp measured pieces
- 1 medium-sized yellow onion, diced (around 1 container)

Method

1. Consolidate all ingredients in slow cooker.
2. Cover, and cook on "low" for 8 hours or until veggies are delicate.
3. To Freeze Consolidate all ingredients (with the exception of chicken stock) in a gallon-sized plastic cooler pack. Evacuate however much air as could reasonably be expected, seal, and stop for up to three months. At the point when prepared to cook, defrost in the fridge overnight and add to slow cooker with chicken soup. Cook on "low" setting for 8 hours or until veggies are delicate.

19. Health Turkey Black Bean Chili

Ingredients

- 1 pound of ground turkey
- 28oz container of tomato sauce
- 2 jars of dark beans (15oz each), depleted and washed
- 1 container of petite diced tomatoes (14.5oz), undrained
- 1 2/3 container solidified corn
- 2 extensive cloves of garlic, minced
- 1 tablespoon paprika
- 1 tablespoon stew powder
- 2 teaspoons ground cumin
- 1/2 teaspoon ground oregano
- 1/4 teaspoon pulverized red pepper drops

Method

1. Add all ingredients to your slow cooker.
2. Cover and cook on low 6-8 hours.
3. Break separated turkey and blend.
4. To Freeze and Cook Later
5. Mark a gallon-sized plastic cooler sack with the name of the formula, cooking guidelines, and use-by date (which would be 3 months from the prep date).
6. Add all ingredients to cooler pack, seal, and stop up to three months.
7. Defrost.
8. Cook on low setting in slow cooker for 6-8 hours.
9. Break separated ground turkey and blend.
10. Present with destroyed cheddar and chips!

20. Delicious Chicken Curry

Ingredients

- 2 pounds boneless, skinless chicken bosoms, cut into nibble size pieces
- 1, 6oz container of tomato glue
- 1, 13.5oz container of coconut milk
- 1 little onion, slashed (around one container)
- 2 measures of solidified peas
- 1, 14.5oz jar of tomato sauce (around 1 3/4 container)
- 2 vast cloves of garlic, minced
- 3 tablespoons nectar
- 2 tablespoons curry powder
- 1 teaspoon salt
- 1 teaspoon pounded red pepper

Method

1. In a dish, join tomato sauce, garlic, nectar, and seasonings. Put aside.
2. Include whatever remains of the ingredients to your slow cooker. Spread with the tomato sauce/flavoring blend.
3. Cook on low 8 hours.
4. To Freeze Join the greater part of the ingredients in a gallon-sized cooler sack and stop for up to three months. At the point when prepared to cook, defrost overnight in your cooler and cook in your slow cooker for 10-12 hours on low. Since the Slow Cooker Chicken Curry cooks without precedent for your slow cooker, it won't suggest a flavor like scraps!
5. Present with white or chestnut rice, and Enjoy!

21. Apricot-Ginger Chicken with Healthy Green Beans

Ingredients

- 1 pound boneless, skinless chicken bosoms (Chicken thighs additionally taste extraordinary)
- 2/3 container apricot jam
- 1 tablespoon low sodium soy sauce
- 1-creep new ginger root, peeled and ground (If you purchase a huge root, you can solidify whatever is remaining. I put the remaining establish entire in my cooler.)
- 3 cloves garlic, peeled and minced
- 1 pound solidified green beans (You can sub new)

Method

1. Consolidate all ingredients in a gallon-sized plastic cooler pack. Evacuate however much air as could reasonably be expected, seal, and lay level in the cooler for up to 3 months.
2. Cook
3. Defrost overnight in cooler or in a dish of icy water. Dump into slow cooker and cook on "low" setting for 6 hours or until chicken is cooked through.
4. Present with quinoa, chestnut rice, potatoes, or whatever you like.

22. Tasty Beef, Lime and Cilantro Chili

Ingredients

- 1 pound incline ground hamburger
- 1, 14.5oz jar of tomato sauce
- 1, 14.5oz jar of petite diced tomatoes, undrained
- 2, 15oz jars dark beans, depleted and flushed
- 1 little onion, slashed (around one container)
- 1 lime
- 2 extensive cloves of garlic, minced
- 1 tablespoon stew powder
- 2 teaspoons ground cumin
- New cilantro, slashed (for garnish)
- Newly destroyed cheddar (for garnish – Optional)

Method

1. Chestnut ground hamburger in a skillet.
2. Empty tomato sauce into a dish and include garlic, stew powder, and ground cumin. Blend to join.
3. Include cooked meat, prepared tomato sauce, jar of diced tomatoes, beans, and onion to your slow cooker.
4. Get-up-and-go the lime and add the get-up-and-go to the slow cooker. Sliced the lime down the middle and add the greater part of its juice to the slow cooker (I suggest crushing over a little strainer or bowl first to get the seeds).
5. Cook on low 8 hours.
6. Present with cleaved, crisp cilantro and destroyed cheddar!

23. Health Split Pea Soup

Ingredients

- 1 lb. dry split peas
- 2 measures of diced turkey bacon, around 8 oz. (or 2 measures of any ham item you have available)
- 1 vast yellow onion, diced
- 1 glass celery, slashed
- 2 glasses carrots, slashed
- 3 cloves of garlic, minced
- 1/2 teaspoon thyme
- 2 narrows clears out
- 32 oz. of chicken juices (here's my natively constructed form)
- 2 containers water

Method

1. Put all ingredients into a 6 quart stewing pot. Spread and cook on LOW for 7-8 hours or on HIGH for 4-5 hours.
2. Stewing pot split Pea Soup - Step 1 - Family Fresh Meals -
3. Here is the turkey bacon I utilized. LOVE this stuff!
4. Stewing pot split Pea Soup - Step 2 - Family Fresh Meals -
5. Expel straight leaves before serving. We want to serve our Crockpot Split Pea Soup with flame broiled cheddar sammies or some warm pieces of bread!

24. Delicious Butter Chicken

Ingredients

- 1 pound boneless skinless chicken bosom, cut into nibble size pieces
- 1/2 onion, finely minced
- 2 tablespoons margarine
- 3 cloves garlic, minced or ground
- 1 tablespoon naturally ground ginger
- 2 teaspoons curry powder
- 1-2 teaspoons curry glue (I utilized Thai Red Curry Paste and 2 teaspoons)
- 2 tablespoons garam masala (Spices)
- 1/2-1 teaspoon turmeric (I utilized 1/2 since my family is not obsessed with turmeric)
- 1 teaspoon cayenne pepper (utilize less in the event that you are not a hot individual)
- 1/4 teaspoon salt
- 1 (6 ounce) can tomato glue
- 1 (14 ounce) can coconut milk, consistent or lite (I utilized normal), in addition to progressively if necessary to thin the sauce
- 1/2 container Greek yogurt (I utilized 0%)
- 1/4 container creamer or substantial cream
- Cooked white rice, for serving
- New custom made Naan, for scooping (an unquestionable requirement!)

Method

1. In a huge glass measuring container or dish combine the coconut milk, Greek yogurt and cream. Blend in the tomato glue, garlic, ginger and all the flavors.
2. Blend well. Spray within your stewing pot dish with cooking shower or oil with olive oil. To the dumbfound sprinkle the onion the base. Include the chicken and

afterward pour the coconut milk blend over the chicken so the chicken is totally secured.

3. Include the spread and place the cover on the slow cooker. Cook on high for 4 hours or on low for 6 to 8 hours. I get a kick out of the chance to mix mine a few times amid cooking, yet it is a bit much. At the point when prepared to serve taste and season with salt and pepper if wanted. Serve over rice with a major bit of new Naan

25. Tuscan Sausage and Healthy White Bean Ragu with Buttered Gnocchi.

Ingredients

- 1/2 of a sweet onion, finely cleaved
- 4 cloves garlic, minced or ground
- 2 (28 ounce) jars entire san Marzano tomatoes
- 3 tablespoons tomato glue
- 1/2 glass red wine
- 2 teaspoons dried basil
- 2 teaspoons dried oregano
- 2 straight clears out
- 1/2 teaspoons salt and pepper
- 1 pound ground zesty Italian frankfurter
- 1 group Tuscan kale, generally slashed
- 3 glasses cooked white beans (around 1 14 ounce can)
- 1 pound gnocchi
- 2 tablespoons margarine
- Crisp basil and parmesan cheddar, for garnish

Method

1. Utilizing your hands, squash the tomatoes over the dish of a 4-8 quart simmering pot. Include the onion, garlic, tomato glue, red wine, dried basil, dried oregano, sound leaves, salt and pepper. Give everything a decent stir.
2. Now snatch the wiener and move it into exceptionally little, nibble size balls, adding the to the stewing pot as you go. The littler you can roll the balls, the better. Delicately mix the hotdog into the sauce. Spread the simmering pot and cook on low for 6-8 hours. 30 minutes before serving, mix in the kale and white beans.
3. Wrench the heat up to high, cover and cook another 20-30 minutes. Meanwhile, cook the gnocchi as indicated by bundle bearings and afterward hurl with 2 tablespoons margarine and somewhat crisp basil + parmesan. To serve,

isolate the gnocchi among plates or bowls. Top with the ragu and afterward decorate with basil and parmesan. Enjoy!

26. Healthy SPINACH ARTICHOKE

Ingredients

- 1 (10 oz.) pack new child spinach, generally hacked
- 1 (13.75 oz.) can quartered artichoke hearts, slashed and depleted
- 1 (8 ounce) block low-fat cream cheddar, cut into 1-inch solid shapes
- 1 glass light sharp cream or plain Greek yogurt
- 1 container destroyed Mozzarella cheddar
- 1/2 container ground Parmesan cheddar
- 1/3 container finely-slashed white or red onion
- 4 cloves garlic, minced
- 1/2 tsp. dark pepper
- 1/4 tsp. salt

Method

1. Consolidate all ingredients in a largeblending bowl and mix until uniformly joined. (You can likewise blend the blend really inside the dish of your slow cooker, however it would be simpler in a largeblending dish.) Transfer the blend to the dish of your slow cooker that has been moistened within in advance with cooking shower.
2. Cook on low for 3-4 hours or on high for 2 hours, or until the plunge is totally warmed through and the cheddar is liquefied. Give the plunge a decent mix and season with additional salt and pepper if necessary.
3. Exchange to a serving dish, and serve warm with chips or bread or pita wafers or whatever scoops you'd like.

27. Italian Chicken and Healthy Broccoli Rabe Chili.

Ingredients

- 3 pounds boneless, skinless chicken thighs or bosoms
- 1 little sweet onion, diced
- 3 cloves garlic, minced or ground
- 2 tablespoons bean stew powder
- 1 tablespoon dried oregano
- 2 teaspoons smoked paprika
- 2 teaspoons dried thyme
- ¼ teaspoon allspice
- ¼-½ teaspoon pulverized red pepper pieces
- 1 dried sound leaf
- 1 teaspoon salt + pepper, or to taste
- 1 (6 ounce) can tomato glue
- 4 mugs low sodium chicken stock
- ½ glass balsamic vinegar
- 1 vast cluster broccoli rabe, closes trimmed + generally hacked
- 1 (12 ounce) jug broiled red peppers, cut
- 1 (15 ounce) can cannellini beans, depleted + flushed
- 1 glass newly ground parmesan cheddar, in addition to additional for serving
- ½ glass hacked parsley, in addition to additional for serving

Method

1. In the dish of a 6-8 quart slow cooker pot, include the chicken, onion, garlic, stew powder, oregano, paprika, thyme, allspice, pulverized red pepper chips, inlet leaf, salt and pepper. Next include the tomato glue, chicken stock and balsamic vinegar.

2. Give everything a tender blend to join. Spread the simmering pot and cook on low for 6 to 8 hours (or 4-6 hours on high) blending more than once if possible. During the most recent 30 minutes of cooking, mix the broccoli rabe, broiled red peppers and cannellini beans together in a dish and add to the slow cooker.
3. Wrench the heat up to high, cover and let cook 20-30 minutes longer. Lightly shred the chicken with two forks, it ought to simply go into disrepair. Blend in the parmesan and parsley. Ladle the soup into dishes and present with parmesan + hard bread for plunging.

28. Healthy Pumpkin Spice Cinnamon Buns

Ingredients

- 3 mugs generally useful flour
- 1/4 container sugar
- 1 bundle dynamic dry yeast
- 1/2 container vanilla almond milk
- 1/4 container water
- 3/4 container pureed pumpkin
- 1/2 glass canola oil
- 1 Flaxseed egg (1 TBS flaxseed to 1/2 TBS warm water, let it sit for 5 minutes)

Filling Ingredients:

- 1/3 glass margarine
- 1/3 glass cocoa sugar
- 2 tsp ground cinnamon
- 2 tsp nutmeg
- 1 tsp ginger
- 1 tsp ground gloves

Icing Ingredients:

- 4 oz. vegetarian cream cheddar, delicate
- 1 glass powdered sugar
- 1/2 stick vegetarian margarine, delicate
- 1/2 tsp vanilla concentrate
- 1/2 tsp lemon juice

Method

1. In a largedish, join flour, sugar and yeast. Fold in almond milk, water, pumpkin, flaxseed egg and oil into attempt ingredients. Structure into a ball and let it sit in dish, secured with a towel, for 30-45 minutes.
2. When mixture has settled, move into a rectangle on a daintily floured surface.

3. Combine filling ingredients and season moved rectangle batter with sugary, pumpkin zest blend. Roll long side to long side, squeeze finishes and after that cut into 12-14 cuts.
4. Place in lubed simmering pot and cook on high for 60-an hour and a half (perform the toothpick test to decide doneness. In the event that it confesses all, you're ready!)
1. Stir up icing/coat and pour over hot moves to make an ooey, gooey, impeccably soggy cinnamon bun. Top with pecan pieces in case you're feeling wild

29. Amazing French toast Casserole

Ingredients

- 2 entire eggs
- 2 egg whites
- 1/2 glasses 1% milk, (almond or soy will likewise work)
- 2 tablespoon nectar
- 1 teaspoon vanilla concentrate
- 1/2 teaspoon cinnamon
- 9 Slices entire grain bread

FILLING:

- 3 containers finely diced uncooked apple pieces (Honey Crisp or Gala are both incredible in this formula)
- 3 tablespoon nectar
- 1 teaspoon lemon juice
- 1/3 container diced crude pecans
- 1/2 teaspoon cinnamon

Method

1. Add the initial 6 ingredients to a medium blending dish, rush to consolidate. Softly splash within the slow cooker with nonstick cooking shower.
2. Include all the filling ingredients in a little blending bowl and mix to coat apple pieces, put aside.
3. Cut bread cuts into triangles (that is down the middle, just triangle formed). Place one layer of bread (6 triangles) on the base of the slow cooker, include ¼ of the filling and rehash until there are 3 layers of bread. Add the remaining filling to the top.
4. Pour egg blend over bread. Cover and cook on high 2 to 2-1/2 or low 4 hours, or until bread has drenched up the fluid.
5. 3 Bananas (diced) can be substituted for apples.

30. Healthy Blueberry and Chia Quinoa

Ingredients

- Soy milk
- Quinoa
- Blueberries
- Chia seeds
- nectar

Method

1. Mix soy milk, water, quinoa, blueberries, chia seeds, and nectar together in a slow cooker.
2. Cook on Low 6 to 8 hours.

31. Healthy Root Vegetable Stew

Ingredients

- 1/4 glass olive oil
- 2 medium yellow onions, substantial craps
- Genuine salt
- 1/4 teaspoons ground ginger
- 1 (3-inch) cinnamon stick
- 1/2 teaspoon ground coriander
- 1/4 teaspoon ground cumin
- 1/8 teaspoon cayenne pepper
- Squeeze saffron strings
- Crisply ground dark pepper
- 1 pound Yukon Gold potatoes (around 3 substantial), extensive craps
- 1 pound carrots (around 4 to 5 medium), peeled and extensive ivories
- 1 pound parsnips (around 4 medium), peeled and vast bones
- 3 mugs low-sodium chicken or vegetable juices
- 2 pounds sugar infant pumpkin or butternut squash (around 1 little), peeled, seeded, and expansive craps
- 1 pound sweet potatoes (around 2 medium), peeled and expansive bones
- 1 (15-ounce) can chickpeas, otherwise called garbanzo beans, depleted and flushed (around 1/2 mugs)
- 1/2 glass brilliant raisins, otherwise called sultanas
- 1 bundle spinach, trimmed and washed (around 4 glasses inexactly stuffed)
- 1/2 tablespoons juice vinegar, in addition to additional as required

Method

1. Heat the oil in an extensive skillet over medium heat until shining. Include the onions and a squeeze of salt and cook over medium heat until translucent, around 4 minutes. Include the ginger, cinnamon, coriander, cumin, cayenne, saffron, and a squeeze of pepper and cook until fragrant, around 1 minute.
2. Transfer the blend to a slow cooker, include the potatoes, carrots, parsnips, and soup, season with salt and pepper, and mix to join. Cover and cook on high for 1/2 hours.
3. Add the pumpkin or squash, sweet potatoes, chickpeas, and raisins, season with salt, and mix to join. Cover and keep on cooking on high until a blade effectively punctures the vegetables, around 2 hours additionally, mixing following 60 minutes. Include the spinach and delicately blend (don't overmix). Let sit until withered. Delicately blend in the vinegar, taste, and season with more salt, pepper, and vinegar as required.

32. Amazing Cajun Stew

Ingredients

- 3/4 pound andouille or kielbasa, cut into 1/2-inch-thick adjusts
- 1 red onion, cut into wedges
- 2 garlic cloves, minced
- 2 celery stalks, coarsely cleaved
- 1 red or green chime pepper, coarsely hacked
- 2 tablespoons generally useful flour
- 1 (28-ounce) can diced tomatoes
- 1/4 teaspoon cayenne pepper
- Coarse salt
- 1/2 pound extensive shrimp, peeled and deveined
- 2 mugs solidified cut okra (from 8-ounce bundle), defrosted

Method

1. In a 5-to-6-quart slow cooker, place wiener, onion, garlic, celery, and chime pepper. Sprinkle with flour and hurl to coat. Include tomatoes and their fluid, 1/2 container water, and cayenne; season with salt. Cover and cook until vegetables are delicate, 3 1/2 hours on high (or 7 hours on low).
2. Include shrimp and okra, cover, and cook until shrimp are misty all through, 30 minutes (or 1 hour on low).

33. Healthy Red Beans and Rice

Ingredients

- 1 tablespoon olive oil
- 1 glass diced yellow onion
- 3/4 slashed red chime pepper
- 1 stalk celery, diced
- 2 cloves garlic, minced
- Legitimate or ocean salt to taste
- 1/4 teaspoon cayenne pepper
- 1/2 teaspoon newly ground dark pepper
- 2 teaspoons newly cut thyme
- 1 inlet leaf
- 2(15 ounce) jars dull red kidney beans
- 3 containers chicken soup (low sodium, fat free)
- 2 containers uncooked long grain chestnut rice

Hotdog INGREDIENTS:

- 1 lb. incline ground turkey or chicken, 93% functions admirably
- 1/2 teaspoon garlic powder
- 1/2 teaspoon ground dark pepper
- 1 teaspoon dried sage
- 1/2 teaspoon red pepper pieces
- 1/4 teaspoon cayenne pepper
- 1 teaspoon dried oregano

Method

For the wiener:

1. Put all the above wiener ingredients into a vast blending bowl and blend altogether until all around mixed. Make into little meatballs, around 1/2". Refrigerate while veggies are cooking.

For the beans:

2. In a substantial skillet, heat olive oil to medium-low, include onions, ringer pepper and celery, sauté until delicate, around 4 minutes. Add garlic and sauté one extra moment. Include sautéed onion, chime pepper, celery, garlic and remaining ingredients to the slow cooker, mix to consolidate.
3. Include wiener meatballs and mix delicately, cover and cook on low 6-8 hours. Prescribe 4-6 quart slow cooker.

For the rice:

4. Independently, cook cocoa rice as indicated by the bearings on bundle.

To serve:

5. Evacuate the cove leaf and serve hotdog meatballs and beans over a bed of cocoa rice.

34. Protein Rich Buffalo Chicken Lettuce

Ingredients

For the chicken:

- 24 oz. boneless skinless chicken bosom
- 1 celery stalk
- 1/2 onion, diced
- 1 clove garlic
- 16 oz. fat free low sodium chicken juices
- 1/2 glass hot cayenne pepper sauce (I utilized Frank's)

For the wraps:

- 6 expansive lettuce leaves, Bibb or Iceberg
- 1/2 glasses destroyed carrots
- 2 expansive celery stalks, cut into 2 inch matchsticks

Method

1. In a slow cooker, join chicken, onions, celery stalk, garlic and juices (enough to cover your chicken, use water if the container of juices isn't sufficient). Cover and cook on high 4 hours.

35. Delicious Turkey Osso Buco

Ingredients

- 1 teaspoon dried thyme
- 2 entire turkey legs (around 3 1/4 pounds all out), cut at joints into drumsticks and thighs, skin evacuated
- 1 tablespoon olive oil
- 2 medium onions, coarsely hacked
- 2 medium carrots, peeled, hacked
- 2 celery stalks, hacked
- 6 garlic cloves, minced, separated
- 1/2 container dry red wine
- 1 28-ounce can diced tomatoes in juice
- 1/4 container cleaved new Italian parsley
- 1 teaspoon ground lemon peel

Method

1. Rub thyme over turkey; sprinkle with salt and pepper. Exchange to 6-quart slow cooker. Heat oil in huge nonstick skillet over medium-high heat. Include onions, carrots, and celery; sauté 8 minutes. Blend in 4 minced garlic cloves. Exchange vegetables to slow cooker. Add wine to skillet; bubble until decreased by 1/3, around 1 minute. Pour wine and tomatoes with juice over turkey. Spread; cook on high until turkey is exceptionally delicate and tumbles off bone, around 5 1/2 hours.
2. Blend parsley, peel, and remaining garlic in dish for gremolata. Utilizing opened spoon, expel turkey from pot. Pull meat from bones; separate meat among 6 bowls. Season sauce with salt and pepper; spoon over turkey. Sprinkle with gremolata.

36.Delicious Tamale Pie

Ingredients

- 1 med. onion, hacked
- 2 C. solidified soy burger disintegrates
- 1 15-oz. can kidney beans, depleted, flushed
- 1 10-oz. can enchilada sauce
- 1 6.5-oz. pocket brilliant corn biscuit and bread blend
- 1/3 C. milk
- 2 Tbs. spread or margarine, liquefied
- 1 egg
- 1/2 C. destroyed Colby-Monterey Jack cheddar mix
- 1 4.5-oz. can slashed green chilies, undrained
- 1/4 C. harsh cream
- 4 med. green onions, slashed

Method

1. Shower 8 inch skillet with cooking splash. Include onion; cook over medium heat around 3 minutes, blending every so often until fresh delicate. In slow cooker, blend disintegrates, onions, beans and enchilada sauce.
2. In medium dish, blend corncake blend, drain, spread and egg just until soaked. Blend in cheddar and chilies. Spoon over blend in slow cooker. Spread; cook on Low heat setting 4 hours 30 minutes to 5 hours 30 minutes or until toothpick embedded in focal point of hoe cake tells the truth. Serve tamale pie with harsh cream and green onions.

37. Healthy Garlic Cauliflower Mashed Potatoes

Ingredient

- 1 head of cauliflower
- 3 containers water
- 4 substantial garlic cloves, peeled
- 1 tsp salt
- 1 straight leaf
- 1 Tbsp. spread
- Milk (if necessary)
- Salt and Pepper

Method

1. Cut the cauliflower into florets and spot in the slow cooker.
2. Include the water, garlic cloves, salt and sound leaf.
3. Cover and cook on HIGH for 2-3 hours or on LOW for 4-6 hours.
4. Expel the garlic cloves and sound leaf. Channel the water.
5. Include the margarine and let it melt.
6. Utilize a potato masher to pound the cauliflower or in the event that you need to utilize a drenching blender to make it more smooth
7. You can do that. On the off chance that it needs drain include it in a tablespoon at once.
8. Salt and pepper to taste. Present with chives or green onions.

38. Tasty Indian Chole

Ingredients

- 2 cups of chickpeas soaked overnight
- 3 cloves garlic, minced
- 1 large onion, minced
- 1 red bell pepper, minced
- 2 14 oz. can of diced tomatoes
- 1-inch piece ginger, minced
- 1 14 oz. can of coconut milk
- 1/2 tsp cayenne pepper
- 1 tsp coriander powder
- 1/2 tsp turmeric
- ½ tsp ground cardamom
- ¼ tsp ground cloves
- 1 tbsp. vegetable oil
- 1 tsp garam masala
- tsp mustard seeds
- 1/2 tsp salt

Method

1. Blend all the ingredients but chickpeas in a food processor or a blender until liquid. Wash and drain chickpeas, place them in a slow cooker, pour the blended mixture over and cook on low for 6-7 hours or on high for 4-5.
2. Make ahead: we usually make double or triple of this recipe, since we love it. Let it cool, and store chole in freezer-safe zip-lock bags in the freezer for up to 6 months.

39. Delicious Brown Rice Pudding

Ingredients

- 2/3 container long grain cocoa rice (My most loved for this formula is Lundberg Long Grain Brown Rice)
- 1 teaspoon cinnamon
- 1/4 container foul sweetener (In this formula we utilized coconut palm sugar. Different choices are sucanat and nectar)
- 1 (13 1/2 ounce) can lite coconut milk
- 1 2/3 container low-fat milk
- 2/3 container raisins (Optional)
- 1 teaspoon unadulterated vanilla concentrate

Method

1. Include rice, cinnamon and sugar to the slow cooker, mix to join. Include both milks, blend to join, cover and cook on low 3-4 hours, or until rice is delicate and fancied thickness has been come to.
2. Just before killing the slow cooker, include vanilla and raisins, blend to consolidate, cover and permit to set around 10 minutes after the slow cooker has been killed. Add extra cinnamon and raisins for topping. Suggest 4-6 quart slow cooker.

40. Healthy Orange Zinger Cheesecake

Ingredients

- 6 graham wafers (entirety)
- non-stick cooking splash
- Filling
- 3/4 container water
- 3 tablespoons cornstarch
- 8 ounces cream cheddar
- 8 ounces tofu (consistent)
- 2/3 container sugar
- 2 tablespoons chestnut sugar
- 1 teaspoon vanilla concentrate
- 1 medium orange, squeezed and zested

Method

1. Pour around some water into slow cooker (1/2-creep) and place trivet or topsy turvy dish into cooker. Spread with top and turn onto high.
2. In the interim, place graham saltines in nourishment processor. Process into pieces (you ought to have around 1 glass). Splash an 8-inch round cake container with vegetable oil shower and place scraps into base of dish, spreading them equally crosswise over base.
3. Mix together the water and cornstarch and spot into blender container. Include remaining filling ingredients, aside from the squeezed orange and get-up-and-go. Mix for 1-2 minutes until smooth, scratching drawbacks of jug with spatula once in a while. At the point when filling is rich, include squeezed orange and pizzazz and prodigy for 3 seconds, until simply consolidated.
4. Pour filling on top of graham saltine scrap outside layer. Place skillet on top of trivet, spread with top and cook for 3 hours on HI. At the point when time is up, expel cover, turn off slow cooker, and permit cake to cool for 30-an hour. At the point when sufficiently cool to handle,

evacuate cake skillet and spot in ice chest to chill, 2-3 hours before serving.

41. Delicious Hot Mocha

Ingredients

- 8 glasses milk
- 1 glass (6-ounce bundle) semisweet chocolate smaller than expected pieces or 6 (1-ounce) semisweet chocolate heating squares, hacked
- 1/2 glass powdered sugar
- 1/4 mug moment espresso granules
- 1 glass schnapps
- Sweetened whipped cream (Optional)
- Ground semisweet chocolate (Optional)

Method

1. Join initial 5 ingredients in a 4-quart slow cooker.
2. Cover and cook on LOW 4 to 5 hours or until completely warmed and chocolate is liquefied, racing following 2 hours. Rush before serving. Present with sweetened whipped cream and ground chocolate, if coveted.

42. Delicious Beer Barbecue Chicken

Ingredients

- 4 Boneless Skinless Chicken Breasts, defrosted
- 18 oz. Sweet Baby Ray's Honey Barbecue Sauce
- 6 oz. Root Beer

Method

1. Cook chicken in stewing pot on HIGH for 3 hours or LOW for 6 hours {covered}
2. Following 3 hours on HIGH or 6 hours on LOW, empty juices out of stewing pot
3. Combine BBQ Sauce and Root Beer in little bowl.
4. Pour blend over chicken, and cook on high for 30 more minutes {covered}

43. Delicious Cranberry Chicken

Ingredients

- 4 Boneless Skinless Chicken Breasts, defrosted
- 1 can Ocean Spray Whole Berry Cranberry Sauce {14 oz.}
- 1 pkg. Dry Onion Soup
- 8 oz. Kraft Catalina Dressing {Russian Dressing can be substituted}

Method

1. Cook chicken in Crockpot on HIGH for 3 hours or LOW for 6 hours {covered}.
2. Following 3 hours on HIGH or 6 hours on LOW, empty juices out of simmering pot.
3. Combine Catalina Dressing, Cranberry Sauce and Dry Onion Soup Mix.
4. Pour blend over chicken, and cook on HIGH for 30 more minutes {covered}, or until done.

44. Amazing Tomato Basil Chicken

Ingredients

- 4 Fresh Boneless Skinless Chicken Breasts {approx. 3 – 3.5 lbs.}
- 1 box Penne Noodles, cooked still somewhat firm
- 1 jug Classic Tomato and Basil Pasta Sauce {16 oz.} – 2 glasses or 480 mL
- 1 glass Shredded Mozzarella Cheese
- 6 cloves Garlic, minced
- 1½ tsp. Onion Powder
- 1 tsp. Oregano
- 1 tsp. Basil
- ½ tsp. Rosemary

Method

1. Place chicken in Crockpot and cook on HIGH for 3 hours or LOW for 6 hours {covered}
2. Following 3 hours on HIGH or 6 hours on LOW, empty juices out of Crock Pot.
3. In little blending dish, consolidate Tomato and Basil Sauce, minced Garlic, Onion Powder, Oregano, Basil, and Rosemary and mix well.
4. Pour sauce blend over chicken, sprinkle with Mozzarella, Cover with top, and Cook for 30 more minutes on HIGH, or until done.
5. While chicken is completing the process of cooking set up the Pasta, cooked still somewhat firm, then serve every chicken bosom with a side of hot pasta. Enjoy!!

45. Delicious Country Style Chicken Recipe!

Ingredients

- 4 Boneless Skinless Chicken Breasts, defrosted
- 1 can Campbell's Chicken Gravy {14.5 oz.}
- 1 parcel Lipton's Onion Soup Mix {dry}
- Pepper to taste

Method

1. Cook chicken in slow cooker on HIGH for 3 hours or LOW for 6 hours {covered}
2. Following 3 hours on HIGH or 6 hours on LOW, empty juices out of slow cooker
3. Combine sauce, dry onion soup blend, and pepper.
4. Pour blend over chicken, and cook on HIGH for 30 more minutes {covered}, or until done. Enjoy!

48. Delicious BBQ Bacon Chicken Sandwiches!

Ingredients

- 4 – 5 Boneless Skinless Chicken Breasts, defrosted
- 1 bottle Guy Fieri Kansas City Barbecue Sauce {19 oz.}
- ½ White Onion, Sliced
- Onion Burger Buns
- Bacon, cooked until fresh

Method

1. Include chicken, BBQ sauce, and cut onions to slow cooker and cook on HIGH for 3.5 hours, or LOW for 7 hours {covered}, or until done.
2. After chicken is cooked, expel from slow cooker and shred utilizing 2 forks.
3. Place a decent estimated part on the base bun of your sandwich, sprinkle with somewhat additional sauce from the simmering pot, and top with Crispy Bacon cuts and top bun. YUM!

49. Healthy Honey Mustard Chicken Recipe!

Ingredients

- 4 Boneless Skinless Chicken Breasts, defrosted
- 1 container French's Dijon Mustard {12 oz.}
- 1/4 container Honey

Method

1. Cook chicken in Crockpot on HIGH for 3 hours or LOW for 6 hours {covered}
2. Following 3 hours on HIGH or 6 hours on LOW, empty juices out of stewing pot
3. Combine Honey and Mustard.
4. Pour blend over chicken, and cook on HIGH for 30 more minutes {covered}, or until done. Enjoy!

50. Amazing Buffalo Ranch Chicken Drumsticks

Ingredients

- Approx. 10 Chicken Drumsticks, defrosted {about 4 lbs.}
- 1 container Frank's Buffalo Red Hot Wings Sauce {12 oz.}
- 1 Hidden Valley Ranch Seasoning Mix bundle (1 oz.) or 3 Tbsps. Buttermilk Ranch Dressing Mix

Method

1. Place Drumsticks in Crockpot.
2. Spread with cover and cook on HIGH for 3 hours.
3. After 3 hours, expel juices from stewing pot.
4. In little blending dish, consolidate Ranch Packet and Buffalo Sauce and mix well.
5. Pour blend over chicken.
6. Cover, and cook for 30 minutes more, or until done.
7. Optional: Garnish with hacked Green Onions

Made in the USA
Coppell, TX
01 January 2025

43773861R00039